Souvenir of
AUSTRALIA

CONTENTS

An Introduction

In 1964, Donald Horne, a Sydney academic, wrote a perceptive appraisal of Australia entitled *The Lucky Country*. The nation has revelled in the title ever since. Horne's book may have targeted the smug complacency of the Australian society but a generation later, compared with most other nations, Australia is indeed lucky. Blessed with a marvellous climate, a unique natural environment and a wealth of natural resources, the island continent of Australia is a prosperous, tolerant, independent nation free of terrorism, civil unrest or vast disparities between wealth and poverty.

Australia is the sixth largest country on earth, yet it has only just over 18 million people. This gives it an average population density of about two persons per km^2. Close to 90 per cent of the population lives in the cities, the overwhelming majority in the south-east corner of the country within 20km of the coast. The two largest cities – Sydney and Melbourne – account for almost one-third of the total population.

Top: *The rainforests near Mossman Gorge in Queensland's Daintree National Park were one of the first areas of Australia to be included on UNESCO's World Heritage List.*

Above: *The Indian Ocean surf tears at the sandstone cliffs of Port Alley in the Kalbarri National Park, 550km to the north of Perth.*

Opposite: *Clumps of tussock grass and snappy gums dot the plains of the Millstream–Chichester National Park in the remote Pilbara region.*

Australia's Landscape

From Deserts to Rainforests

For most outsiders, their overwhelming impression of the Australian landscape is of beaches and the outback. In a land that spans 7 682 300km² (approximately 24 times the size of the British Isles) and has a climate that ranges from sub-zero to over 40°C, the features that make up this remarkable country are diverse and quite often contrast with and contradict each other.

The most prominent characteristic of the east coast of Australia is the Great Dividing Range, a chain of low, forested mountains that extends the length of the country from Queensland's Cape York to Wilson's Promontory in Victoria. Forming part of the range are the scenic treasures of Queensland's Glasshouse Mountains, Victoria's Snowy Alps and New South Wales's Blue Mountains. Nestled at Sydney's back door, the Blue Mountains comprise a majestic region of rippling, timbered sandstone hills dissected by vast chasms where waterfalls tumble from the rims of cliffs and disappear in olive-green forests.

To the east of this range, the fertile coastal plain varies from less than 1km to more than 250km in width. The eastern seaboard was once heavily rain-forested and a few pockets remain, especially in the far north Queensland coastal area.

On the western slopes of the Great Divide lies a broad band of fertile grazing country that gives way to broadacre farms of cereal crops and cotton. Further to the west, the land becomes drier, each town is further apart and finally, trees and fences disappear altogether. Here the Australian interior looms like a biblical, shrivelled antiquity that has left the country squeezed of every drop of moisture. The leaves of the eucalypts seem to droop in sullen, exhausted clumps; the soil appears sunburnt and parched; and the rocks look charred with age. Even the seasons seem blurred since most of the plants and trees are non-deciduous. But Australians have affectionate names for the arid interior of their continent: the outback, the dead heart or just simply the centre.

On the western front is a huge shield, in the form of a series of plateaux, comprised of rocks at least 1500 million years old. This vast crustal block leads to the rugged coastline which – along with fertile pockets, pristine beaches and forested havens, most protected as national parks – extends around the country.

Above: *Forests near Manjimup in Western Australia still under-pin the economy of the south-west. The region is known as Tall Timber Country for its giant karri trees which grow up to 60m high.*

Above: *The dome-shaped Bungle Bungle Range rises from the desert in Purnululu National Park.*

Above: *The barren, desiccated hills of the Hamersley Range in Western Australia's Pilbara region provide vivid evidence of the ancient landscape. This area has one of the world's richest iron ore deposits.*

Right: *These rugged cliffs confronting the Great Southern Ocean lie within the Fitzgerald River National Park, the first area in Western Australia listed as a biosphere reserve.*

A Stable Geology

Although Australia is bordered by areas of intense geological turmoil – Papua New Guinea to the north and New Zealand to the south-east – the continent is extremely stable for such a vast landmass. It has no active volcanoes and earth-quakes are rare. Its most destructive natural phenomena are the hurricane-like cyclones that roar in from the sea every year and wreak havoc on stretches of tropical real estate.

Without volcanoes or colliding tectonic plates to build mountains, the landscape is characterised by its flatness. Australia's highest peak, Mount Kosciusko in south-eastern New South Wales, measures just 2230m. Those mountain ranges that once existed have been ground to stumps by aeons of wind and rain. Uluru, close to the centre of the continent, is a chunk of spectacularly eroded sandstone formed 600 million years ago when this area lay at the bottom of the sea.

Australia is also the driest inhabited continent on the planet. Only about one-fifth of the entire landmass receives more than 40cm of rainfall per year, yet the continent was once covered with lush rainforests. Cradled between towering sandstone walls, Palm Valley in Finke Gorge, south-west of Alice Springs, is thickly clothed with red-leaved palms (*Livistona mariae*), a reminder of the time when the interior of the continent was much wetter than it is today.

The twin factors of age and erosion have given Australia some of its most spectacular landscapes. Stretching north from Gulf St Vincent in South Australia, the Flinders Ranges is the most captivating outback park in the country. Here an ancient seabed has been sculpted by the elements into a fractured, fur-rowed landscape of deep valleys, covered with twisted cypress pines, which drop away into creeks lined with river red gums.

A Unique Natural Heritage

Australia's plants and animals are among nature's oddest creations. So weird is its flora and fauna that until 1912 (when the German astronomer Alfred Wegener proposed the theory of continental drift, and fossilised forests were discovered that established a link between Australia, South America, India, South Africa and Antarctica), it was believed that Australia's species had evolved separately from the rest of the planet.

After the disintegration of the supercontinent Gondwana – which once fused Africa, South America, India, Antarctica and Australia – between 45 and 110 million years ago, Australia's life forms developed special characteristics to adapt to the rigours of the climate. In times of drought, the waterholding frog (*Cyclorana platycephala*) locks itself away in an underground chamber, where it remains in a state of suspended animation waiting for rain for up to seven years. Despite its ferocious appearance, the heavy armour of the desert-dwelling thorny devil (*Moloch horridus*) gives it an enormous surface area on which dew condenses; this is then fed into its mouth through an intricate network of capillaries. Several plants, like some members of the hakea family, depend on bushfires – a fact of life in Australia's tinderbox forests – to crack open their seed pods and release the next generation.

Plants and animals that fell prey to predators in other parts of the globe have survived and evolved separately in Australia. These include the marsupials – kangaroos, koalas, numbats, wombats and quolls – and the egg-laying platypus and echidna.

Right:
Found only in Western Australia, the red and green kangaroo paw is the state's floral emblem.

Above: *Contrary to popular opinion, koalas are not bears. They feed only on certain types of eucalypt.*

Above: *The thorny devil is a slow-moving desert-dweller which exists on ants and termites.*

Right: *The royal hakea (Hakea victoriae) is a native of Western Australia and has a woody, nut-like fruit and tough leaves.*

Below: *The platypus is rarely seen in the wild and is one of only three monotremes (egg-laying mammals) which are endemic to Australia and southern New Guinea.*

Opposite:
Found in a vast range of habitats, from Cape York to southern Tasmania, the wallaby is smaller than its relative, the kangaroo.

Left: An Aboriginal woman digs for witchetty grubs in the desert near Alice Springs. Traditional food sources still play an important role in the diet of many Aborigines in the Central Desert.

Australia's People

The Earliest Inhabitants

Like the land they inhabit, the aboriginal people of Australia were once vastly removed from the rest of the world by character as well as distance. Australia's Aborigines are thought to have originated from southern Asia, migrating at a time when the seas were lower and the journey could be made in a series of inter-island voyages. Estimates of the date of their arrival retreat further into the past as new archaeological finds are discovered every decade, but artefacts found in northern Australia suggest that they reached the coast as long as 60 000 years ago – a time when Neanderthals still populated parts of northern Europe.

Above: Warradjan Cultural Centre in Kakadu National Park is a showcase for traditional Aboriginal lifestyle and culture.

Before the coming of Europeans, Aborigines were hunter-gatherers and often nomadic, moving in search of food sources. They lived mostly in clan groups, sharing their food and tools. They had no use for the wheel or money, they worked no metals, they had no alphabet or agriculture and no domesticated animals. However, they adapted superbly to the rigours of their environment. The bark fishing canoes used by Sydney's Iora people – flimsy and unseaworthy according to early diarists – could be made by a single tribesman in a day. Their mastery of the natural resources, such as resin from the spinifex plant (essential for bonding spearheads to shafts), enabled them to populate areas where unsupported Europeans have never established settlements. And while the convict settlers of the First Fleet teetered on the brink of starvation, well-fed Aborigines looked on – probably in amazement.

Below: Kakadu National Park displays many fine examples of Aboriginal art, like those at Ubirr Rock where some paintings date back thousands of years while others are from this century.

They also evolved a complex mythology and spirituality. The cave paintings in Kakadu National Park and Arnhem Land in the Northern Territory document a rich culture of legends and dreams that stretches back for more than 40 000 years – the longest continuous stream of creative expression found on the planet.

From the first day of white settlement, however, the relationship between Aborigines and the new settlers was characterised by homicidal misunderstanding. As the bounds of the colony expanded, the loss of the Aborigines' traditional hunting grounds led inevitably to friction that continued well into the 20th century.

Since the 1970s, political activism among Aborigines and the changing attitudes of the wider community have swung the pendulum of concern. Affirmative action policies have provided funds for Aboriginal health, welfare and employment and recent judicial decisions have supported the principle of Aboriginal land rights pre-dating European colonisation. One of the success stories of Aboriginal self-employment has been in the tourism industry. The chance to discover the rainforests of far north Queensland with an Aboriginal guide or to dig for honey ants with the Pitjantjatjara people in the desert around Uluru offers unforgettable insights into the special relationship between a people and their land.

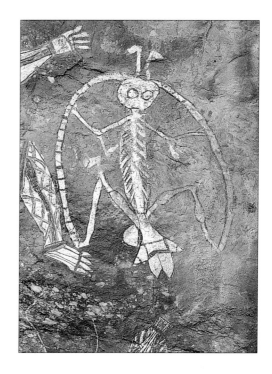

Above: Namarrgon, 'the Lightning Man' on the walls of Nourlangie Rock, is a potent Aboriginal creation spirit-being. His power is manifested in the tremendous lightning storms that sweep Kakadu.

The Arrival of the Europeans

Australia came late to the European consciousness. *Terra Australis Incognita*, the 'Unknown Southern Land' which had teased the imaginations of European geographers for centuries, had certainly been seen by European navigators in the 17th century, and probably by Macassan and Chinese traders long before that.

Motivated more by trade than territorial expansion, early European contacts with Australia were brief and unpromising. The Dutch sea captains Willem Jansz, Dirk Hartog and Abel Janszoon Tasman came, saw and caught the trade winds back out to sea, preferring the vast and far more measurable treasures of the nearby Spice Islands instead. It wasn't until 1770, when Captain James Cook charted the eastern seaboard of the continent, claimed the land on behalf of Great Britain and declared it *terra nullius* (a land untouched by civilisation), that any real interest was shown in the land on the other side of the world.

Left: The Zuytdorp Cliffs, just south of the town of Denham, present a stern brow to the Indian Ocean and are named after the Dutch ship wrecked there in 1712.

Left: Botany Bay was intended to be the settlement site for the First Fleet in 1788, but the lack of fresh water forced them to sail north into Port Jackson.

European Colonisation

On 26 January 1788, a fleet of 11 transport vessels under the command of Captain Arthur Phillip of the Royal Navy sailed into Port Jackson, the site of the present-day city of Sydney. It was not a happy beginning: the first settlers were not escapees from religious or ideological persecution but convicts, flushed from the jails of England.

Below: The University of Sydney was founded in 1852, the first in the colony, and was constructed largely in the Gothic-Revival style fashionable at the time.

For the most part the convicts and their keepers had little agricultural experience, and for several years the infant colony languished on the brink of starvation. The first attempts to grow crops on the sandy soil at Farm Cove – ironically, now the site of Sydney's lush Royal Botanic Garden – failed miserably. It was not until 1791, when James Ruse, a farmer in his native Cornwall, established the first successful farm west of Sydney, that the colony showed any hope that it might be able to feed itself.

By the early 1800s it was recognised that Australia was eminently suited to the production of fine wool. This sparked a boom of exploration and development to supply the textile mills of England, which had themselves been galvanised by the technological advances of the industrial revolution.

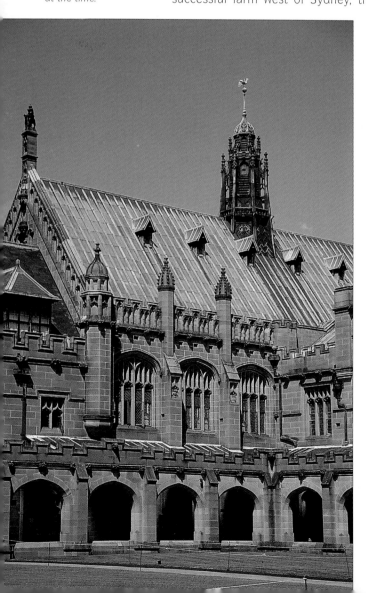

The discovery of gold in 1851 gave the colony its first real flush of prosperity. In the following decade the population trebled; between 1850 and 1890 Sydney and Melbourne founded universities modelled on Oxford and Cambridge and both cities built lavish art galleries and museums. Australia's own manufacturing industry took root and many of the country's most impressive stately homes date from the second half of the 19th century. During this period the first Chinese immigrants arrived, drawn by the prospect of vast riches to be won from the mines, but their welcome was often bad-tempered and bloody, and anti-Chinese riots occurred on several goldfields.

Above: This replica of the Endeavour, the converted Whitby collier in which intrepid Captain James Cook charted much of the east coast, is 32m long.

By the second half of the century, the individual states had already achieved a considerable measure of independence from Great Britain. As early as 1855 they were given the right to elect the lower house of their own two-chamber parliaments. In 1901, the states of the Commonwealth of Australia were joined in a federation. Each state preserves control over important areas such as police, judiciary and education, while responsibilities for taxation, defence, foreign affairs and other aspects of national concern fall within the realm of the federal government.

Left: The present-day face of Australia is no longer Anglo-Irish but one of a wide racial mix. The country is remarkably free of overt racial tensions.

Australians at War

World War I crucially altered the Australian identity. Traditionally, Australia owed its allegiance to Great Britain, yet during the war the country rigorously asserted its independence, placing its troops under Australian rather than British command and demanding an appropriate strategic role for their officers in the conduct of the war. Some 330 000 Australians served in World War I, every one of them a volunteer since the issue of conscription was defeated twice in national referendums. The bloody landing at Gallipoli in southern Turkey is commemorated on Anzac Day, a national holiday when Australia honours the memory of the men and women who have served in the armed forces.

Yet the psychic umbilical cord that bound Australia to Britain was not severed. When Prime Minister Robert Menzies announced in 1939 that 'Great Britain is at war, therefore Australia is at war', the assertion went unchallenged. Australian casualties were less in World War II than the previous conflict but its proximity made the experience more traumatic: Darwin was bombed and Japanese miniature submarines infiltrated Sydney Harbour. Japanese troops came close to conquering all of Papua New Guinea, which could have provided a base for the invasion of Australia.

In the aftermath of World War II, the nation has realigned its allegiance in favour of the United States. This military alliance was underlined when Australia sent troops to fight in Vietnam, a conflict in which 423 Australian service personnel were killed.

Below: Stained-glass windows in the War Memorial's Hall of Memory evoke the reverence with which Australians remember those who died.

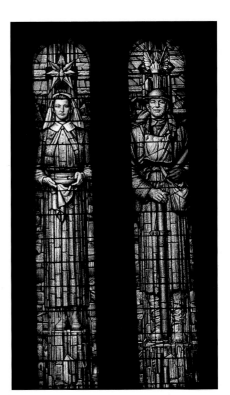

Above: 'Simpson and his Donkey' is a symbol of comradeship and courage. Private John Simpson transported casualties upon Duffy from the battlefields of Gallipoli to safety, until he himself was killed.

Left: Chinese joss houses are now a common sight in Australia and are indicative of how the community has successfully embraced multiculturalism.

Australia Today

Times of Change

Since 1945 the country's population has undergone fundamental changes. Over the past half-century, Australia's original Anglo-Irish population base has been enriched by waves of immigrants from Italy, Greece, Eastern Europe, Lebanon, China and South-East Asia. The effects of this racial inter-mingling have been profound. Today, half of all Australians were either born overseas or have at least one parent who was. Sydney's St Patrick's Day Parade is second only to New York's in size, and parts of Sydney and Melbourne are linguistic enclaves of Greeks, Chinese or Vietnamese.

The effects of migration have had particular impact on the national tastebuds. 'Migrants are Australia's most important gastronomic resource,' according to Stephanie Alexander, one of the country's most influential chefs. What Australia eats now is often described as fusion food – a collage of culinary influences that throws in a splash of olive oil with one hand while tossing in a handful of chopped coriander and chillies with the other.

Above: The various ethnic strands that make up the fabric of modern Australia are encouraged to maintain their identity. This folk troupe entertains crowds in Brisbane's Queen Street Mall.

A Vibrant Economy

Australia has been generously endowed. The continent has enormous reserves of bauxite, nickel, iron ore, coal, gold, oil and natural gas. The country also has one of the world's largest supplies of uranium, although its exploitation has been limited by the anti-nuclear lobby. These riches are the major contributor to Australia's relatively high standard of living. It is thanks to this natural bounty of coal and iron ore, especially, that Australia is one of the only countries that maintains a favourable balance of trade with Japan.

The fracturing of the world into regional economic blocs has forced Australia to develop new relationships and, in the 1990s, the country is working hard to integrate itself with the economies of Asia and to divest itself of some of the remaining links with Great Britain. Recent governments have become aware that they cannot forever base the national income on what Australians dig out of the ground or shear from a sheep's back, and serious efforts are being made to improve Australia's technological sophistication – to become 'the clever country' (a pun on the title of Donald Horne's book) in political parlance.

Above: Dampier on the north coast of Western Australia is the main port in the region, and giant ore carriers dock here to collect minerals.

The Future

As the century draws to a close, Australia is still a constitutional monarchy under the nominal leadership of the reigning British monarch but, increasingly, it is a restless subject. The governor-general, the monarch's representative in Australia, still has important constitutional powers, including the power to dismiss a government. Many Australians regard these powers as a colonial hangover, no longer appropriate for an assertive, independent nation, and one increasingly populated by a people with no ancestral ties to the United Kingdom. The Australian flag – which still incorporates the Union Jack in one corner – causes particular heartache. The movement towards a republic, which would sever forever the constitutional links with Britain, gathers momentum year by year.

Australia also has a major international event with which to celebrate the end of the 20th century. Sydney will host the 2000 Olympic Games, and in Australia, when sport and nationalism combine on such a vast scale, the party promises to last until well into the next century.

Above: The Australian flag incorporates the stars of the Southern Cross as well as the Union Jack, a symbol which many Australians would like to see removed.

Below: Fireworks over Sydney Harbour usher in the New Year, a celebration that has become a tradition.

NEW SOUTH WALES

For most visitors, their first glimpse of Australia will be of the rooftops of Sydney, the country's major international gateway. Wrapped around a glorious harbour, Sydney, the capital of New South Wales, is the biggest, oldest and most cosmopolitan city in Australia. In addition to its natural credentials – including fabulous beaches and a sunny Mediterranean climate – Sydney has a relaxed lifestyle and a multicultural population that gives it the vivacity that is its signature. Sydney is also Australia's premier city – it has the most luxurious real estate, the tallest buildings and the most active nightlife in the country.

The city is also the gateway to the diverse splendours of New South Wales. The stylised figures of an Aboriginal rock painting, the boom of the big Pacific rollers on a honey-coloured stretch of sand, the cackle of a kookaburra in a eucalypt forest, a waratah in flower – these sensations belong to the state. You only have to drive an hour out of Sydney into the Blue Mountains, the Southern Highlands or the Hunter Valley to experience the sights and sounds of the country regions and wilderness.

Above: *Apartment blocks press hard against the beachfront of Manly, one of Sydney's most popular residential and holiday locations.*

Right: *The monorail glides through the canyons of the city overlooked by the Sydney Tower, a 325m spike topped by a golden minaret.*

Left: *Sydney Opera House, built entirely from the proceeds of state-run lotteries, was designed by the inspired Jørn Utzon, a Danish architect selected from an international competition.*

Opposite: *The Sydney Harbour Bridge spans one of the world's greatest harbours, and links the northern and southern shores.*

Above: *Sydney's Harbour Bridge and Opera House are both monumental feats of engineering and have become Australian icons.*

Below: *Replicas of tall-ship masts frame Campbells Storehouse, which is now home to harbourfront restaurants.*

Above: *Spectators line the foreshores for the start of the annual Sydney to Hobart Ocean Yacht Race.*

Opposite: *Famous Bondi Beach is where Sydney takes off its shirt and most of its inhibitions.*

Left: *The Gay and Lesbian Mardi Gras is a celebration of gay pride and attracts visitors from around the globe to take part in the revelry.*

Right: *A striking pagoda marks the entrance to Dixon Street, the centre of Sydney's bright, bustling Chinatown.*

Overleaf: *The city's ferries churn the waters of Sydney Cove, where the history of modern Australia began with the First Fleet in 1788.*

Above: *The Chinese Garden is a tranquil refuge with stylised waterfalls, ponds, rocks and pavilions evoking nature's many moods.*

Above: *The SS* South Steyne, *a former Sydney ferry which is now permanently moored in Darling Harbour, serves as the Olympic Showcase and Information Centre.*

Top: *The Sydney Aquarium located on the foreshore of Darling Harbour displays fascinating exhibits of Australia's marine life, including the dreaded shark.*

Right: *St Mary's Cathedral is the focal point for the city's Roman Catholics and overlooks Hyde Park, a green oasis in the city centre.*

Opposite: *The ornate sandstone facade of the Queen Victoria Building, once the city's produce market, was renovated in the 1980s and now houses an elegant, multi-level shopping plaza.*

Opposite: *The Three Sisters dominate the Jamison Valley; they are viewed at their most majestic angle from Echo Point in Katoomba.*

Above: *Grazing lands extend below the Blue Mountains; the rugged peaks presented a formidable barrier to early explorers.*

Below: *Tyrrells Winery is still operated by the descendants of one of the original wine-makers of the lower Hunter Valley, the state's premier wine-growing region.*

Above: *The Imperial Hotel with its Victorian facade is a favourite weekend escape in the Blue Mountains for Sydney residents.*

Right: *Streams cascade through the Valley of the Waters, one of the loveliest forest glades in the Blue Mountains.*

Above: *The rolling pastures of the Bega Valley are typical of the South Coast region of New South Wales.*

Below: *This grand building is a police station in the Southern Highlands' town of Bowral, a cool-climate area where English-style gardens erupt in a blaze of colour in spring and autumn.*

Opposite: *These white sands are found at Jervis Bay's Iluka Beach, a quiet and relatively unspoilt inlet on the coastline south of Sydney.*

Below: *The tranquil wharves at Twofold Bay, where the town of Eden stands on the southern New South Wales coast, were home to a bustling whaling station at the turn of the century.*

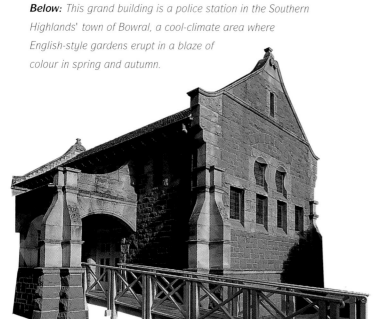

Above: *Hampden Bridge was built in 1898 and spans the Shoalhaven River near the village of Kangaroo Valley in the Southern Highlands.*

24

Above: The once-flourishing koala population of Australia has been depleted by bushfires, attacks from domestic dogs, and roadworks which have cut across koala habitats. The Billabong Breeding Centre at Port Macquarie is one of many institutes helping to prevent their extinction.

Above: Fishing is popular on the north coast of New South Wales because of the easy access to rivers, lakes and ocean shores.

Right: The Pacific Ocean surf curls against the sand of a Port Macquarie beach; a pristine strip of sand is regarded as a birthright of every Australian.

AUSTRALIAN CAPITAL TERRITORY

Canberra, the nation's capital, is a handsome, landscaped city that strikes a bold stance amid the rugged glories of southern New South Wales. From its inception Canberra, within the Australian Capital Territory, was a totally planned city. Designed by the American-born Walter Burley Griffin, the result is a capital of calm and poise generously endowed with parks and gardens. In addition, Canberra's galleries, museums, libraries, sporting academy and technical institutions are a proud display of Australian excellence.

The mountain ranges and forested river valleys that ring the city, combined with a climate that brings warm summers and crisp winters, give Canberra a huge choice of outdoor activities that can be easily enjoyed by visitors.

Above: The High Court of Australia casts an authoritarian reflection across the waters of Canberra's Lake Burley Griffin.

Opposite: Hot-air balloons reveal the full glory of Griffin's vision as they glide over the capital on their daily sunrise adventures.

Below: Canberra is the seat of Australia's federal parliament and the new Parliament House was completed in 1988. The hill on the site was carved away and grass slopes were placed on top of the new building so that it had the same elevation as the old hill, thus retaining the aesthetic tone of the city.

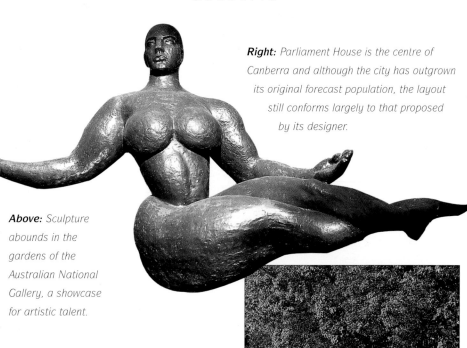

Right: *Parliament House is the centre of Canberra and although the city has outgrown its original forecast population, the layout still conforms largely to that proposed by its designer.*

Above: *Sculpture abounds in the gardens of the Australian National Gallery, a showcase for artistic talent.*

Below: *Cockington Green is a slice of English country life recreated in miniature on the outskirts of Canberra.*

Above: *Canberra is renowned for its parks and gardens. In autumn a molten glow highlights the beauty of Commonwealth Park, while the festival of Floriade celebrates the full colour of spring.*

Below: *Cruise boats meander across Lake Burley Griffin, created by damming the Molonglo River to form the scenic centrepiece of the national capital.*

QUEENSLAND

Queensland is the second largest state in Australia and boasts some of its most important holiday playgrounds. The Gold Coast, just north of the New South Wales border, is superbly equipped with resorts, wildlife parks and aquariums, sports facilities, golden beaches and a fabulous line-up of after-dark entertainment. To the north is the Sunshine Coast, characterised by its marvellous beaches and barefoot lifestyle. Perhaps the most stunning and popular areas are the tropical rainforests of the north and the dazzling coral islands and resorts of the Great Barrier Reef, one of nature's masterworks.

The Queensland capital, Brisbane, combines the thrusting vitality of a modern, energetic city with a sociable country atmosphere. Set on the banks of the meandering Brisbane River, close to the waters of Moreton Bay, it is a city of grace and charm with a balmy, subtropical climate. But don't be misled by its languid pace – this is a city that enjoys the good life, as its restaurants and vibrant cultural venues prove.

Above: *Riverboats tethered on the Brisbane River lie in the shadow of the city's office towers. Brisbane underwent an urban renaissance in the 1980s which brought new vigour to the city.*

Below: *The Shrine of Remembrance in Anzac Square, Brisbane, was built in 1930 to honour the Australians who served in World War I.*

Opposite: *Hamilton Island is the largest of the resorts that have sprung up on the islands of the Whitsunday Passage.*

Above: *South Bank Riverside Markets are held on Stanley Street on one of the glittering waterfront plazas that have become a hall-mark of Brisbane's riverfront.*

Above: *Some of the most popular attractions on the Gold Coast are the theme parks. Warner Bros Movie World is the only movie theme park outside the United States.*

Below: *The Sheraton Mirage has its own marina and is one of the finest of the glittering resort hotels that line the coast.*

Bottom: *The giant loops of the 'Thunderbolt' at the Dreamworld theme park throw down a challenge to thrill-seekers.*

Right: *Apartment blocks overlook the beach at Surfers Paradise, for many visitors an area that is synonymous with holidays and nightlife.*

Opposite: *The wreck of the* Maheno *lies stranded on Fraser Island, the world's largest sand island. Fraser boasts freshwater lakes, forests, spectacular dune formations, superb fishing and wonderful beaches.*

Below: *The impressive butterfly collection at Rockhampton's Botanic Gardens rivals the marine colours of the Great Barrier Reef.*

Above: *The 140km stretch of beaches on Fraser Island attracts thousands of four-wheel-drive enthusiasts; it is one of the few parts of the coast that allows these vehicles unrestricted access.*

Below: *Rockhampton's Botanic Gardens is one of the highlights of this city, which lies on the Tropic of Capricorn. The town is also known as the beef capital of Australia.*

Below: *Outrigger canoes line the beach at Noosa Heads on Queensland's Sunshine Coast, one of the country's most upmarket holiday playgrounds.*

Right: *The pool area at the Hamilton Island resort epitomises the relaxed atmosphere of the island, which boasts the Whitsundays' only jet airport and high-rise complex.*

Below: *Shute Harbour is the mainland gateway to the holiday islands of the Whitsunday Passage. The town's marinas are the base for boat operators who provide charter yachts to visitors in Australia's premier cruising waters.*

Above: *Magnum's is one of the many restaurants and pubs at Airlie Beach, a town near Shute Harbour. Hotels and motels have mushroomed in this area and they provide a less expensive alternative to the island resorts of the Whitsunday Passage.*

Opposite: *The Whitsunday Islands dissolve in shades of aquamarine into the coral seas that surround them. Named by Captain James Cook, these islands were once part of the mainland but 'drowned' when the seas rose at the end of the last ice age.*

Overleaf: *The sparkling sands of Whitehaven Beach on Whitsunday Island are three nautical miles of pure white silica, and a favourite anchorage for sun-worshipping sailors.*

Above: The mottled, peacock colours of the Great Barrier Reef are formed by billions of tiny coral polyps that have created an underwater world teeming with marine life.

Below: Palm Cove, a popular winter holiday destination, is one of the beach resorts along the coast north of Cairns.

Right: A native fig anchors itself to the rocks in defiance of the surging waters of Mossman River, a spectacular torrent that carves its way through the tropical rainforest.

Below: The Kuranda train chugs along the edge of an escarpment on its scenic journey between Cairns and Kuranda.

Right: A bungy jumper prepares for the moment of truth at Smithfield Heights on the northern outskirts of Cairns.

Opposite: There are 340 species of coral making up the vast ecosystem of the Great Barrier Reef, an underwater world of surreal colours almost unknown above the surface.

Above: *An abseiler descends alongside a waterfall in the beautiful Lamington National Park to the west of the Gold Coast.*

Right: *Snorkellers enjoy the waters at Lady Musgrave Island, one of the most southerly of the Great Barrier Reef's coral cays and also the breeding platform for thousands of migratory seabirds as well as turtles which drag themselves ashore to lay their eggs in the sand.*

Below: *Cruising out to the Great Barrier Reef on a daytrip is perhaps one of the most idyllic holiday pastimes in far north Queensland.*

NORTHERN TERRITORY

Darwin, the capital of the Northern Territory, is a bustling, vigorous city that has been enriched by its multicultural population. Despite its turbulent history – the city was bombed by the Japanese in World War II and flattened by Cyclone Tracy on Christmas Eve in 1974 – Darwin is dynamic and has a young and vibrant population. More than any other capital city in the country, its pioneering spirit is never far from the surface.

Darwin is surrounded by pristine tropical wilderness. To the east is Kakadu National Park, the first area in Australia to be included on the World Heritage list. To the south is Alice Springs, a modern, big-hearted oasis with a character all of its own and rich in reminders of the time when this was a frontier town. Alice Springs is also a cultural centre for the Aboriginal people of the Central Desert and a gateway to one of Australia's greatest wonders – the Uluru–Katatjuta National Park.

Right:
Frangipanis
brighten
Darwin's
Botanic Gardens.

Top: *Darwin's tropical Fannie Bay is a wonderful spot for watching the sun set beyond the horizon of the Timor Sea.*

Opposite: *Katatjuta means 'many heads', a reference to the dome shape of these sandstone monoliths which tower above the desert south-west of Alice Springs.*

Above: *Darwin is Australia's most northerly city and its harbour is now an important link in developing trade with Asian countries.*

Right: *The markets at Darwin's Mindil Beach are a great place to meet the locals, who gather in the balmy evenings to sample the multicultural mix of cuisine.*

Left: *Cruise boats travel along Yellow Waters, a freshwater lagoon on the South Alligator River in Kakadu National Park. It provides a habitat for crocodiles, fish and thousands of exotic birds.*

Opposite: *Sandstone outcrops, such as these at Ubirr, provided Aborigines with well-protected shelters; the rock walls also became the canvas for their art.*

Below: *The brolga, an elegant stork-like bird, is found on the swampy margins of creeks and wetlands in the Northern Territory.*

Above: *Canoe trips are certainly the best way to explore spectacular Katherine Gorge, sculpted over many millions of years by the Katherine River as it forged its passage through the majestic sandstone walls to the south of Darwin.*

Below: *Rocky platforms provide perfect lookouts at Ubirr and allow visitors to grasp the vastness of the flood plains of the Kakadu National Park. The Magela plain is one of the many sites within the park where Aboriginal rock art can be found.*

Below: *The red kangaroo is the largest of Australia's marsupials and, like this one's feathered friend, has adapted superbly to the country's environment.*

Above: Katatjuta radiates the light from the dying sun and, like Uluru, changes its mood according to the weather and the time of day.

Right: Uluru is an Australian national icon and a natural wonder that resonates with an almost mystical force. It is not surprising that the Aborigines consider it to be of great spiritual importance.

Above: Alice Springs, the heart of the red centre, lies in the shadow of the MacDonnell Ranges. Despite its modern conveniences, life here still has a pioneering quality.

Right: The Devils Marbles are giant granite tors strewn among hummock grass near the Stuart Highway north of Alice Springs. According to Aboriginal legend, these are the eggs of the Rainbow Serpent, the premier creation spirit of Aboriginal mythology.

Above: Highways seem purposeful as they head off into the distance, but the nearest town could be thousands of kilometres away.

Below: Camels provide a great way to explore the terrain around 'the Alice' and were imported, together with their handlers, from the Indian subcontinent in the 1800s.

WESTERN AUSTRALIA

Perth, the gateway to the west, lies on the banks of the Swan River, which flows generously towards the Indian Ocean. The city is blessed with sparkling beaches, a sunny Mediterranean climate and is surrounded by vineyards. Perth has a relaxed, easy-going lifestyle and it is hardly surprising that one in every four families owns a boat – if you happen to take a weekend cruise on the Swan River, you might well believe that every one of them is out for the day.

Even by Australian standards, Western Australia is huge. The state measures more than 2.5 million km² – larger than all but about a dozen countries – and it includes a vast diversity of terrains, from the scorched red tracts of the Gibson Desert to the pearling and resort town of Broome in the far north, the surreal domes of the Bungle Bungle Range and the giant karri forests and lush vineyards of the Margaret River region.

Top: The skyline of Perth is framed by the Narrows Bridge, which spans the Swan River.

Below: Rottnest Island is a popular weekend escape for Perth residents.

Opposite: Sunset brings a warm glow to Perth's skyline. The city's office towers are the headquarters for many of Australia's giant mineral-exploration companies.

Above: Wildflowers annually spread a carpet of colour across Kings Park, which overlooks Perth and the Swan River environs from its hillside perch.

Right: Fremantle, less than 20km from Perth, is one of Western Australia's biggest attractions with its outdoor cafes, historic buildings and yacht marinas.

Above: The giant red tingle tree is the largest butted eucalypt in the world; towering examples are found in south-west Australia.

Above: Margaret River's vineyards now flourish across hillsides that once formed part of rolling dairy country.

Above: Built at the turn of the century, the York Hotel in Kalgoorlie hints at the fanciful tastes that were spawned by the gold rush.

Opposite: The Nullarbor cliffs meet the Great Australian Bight with dramatic suddenness at the southern edge of the continent.

Below: A road sign on the Nullarbor indicates a trio of unusual hazards.

Below: The beaches at the isolated agricultural service centre of Esperance mark the western border of the Great Australian Bight.

Below: *The Argyle Diamond Mine in the north of Western Australia is the world's largest – the gems recovered from it have made a valuable contribution to the state economy.*

Right: *Dolphins, accustomed to the presence of humans, swim into the shallows to frolic with visitors at Monkey Mia, creating a successful tourism industry in this small, isolated community.*

Opposite: *Weird, spiky limestone knobs, commonly known as the Pinnacles, dot the sands of Nambung National Park north of Perth.*

Above: *Palm Resort at Cable Beach is a composite of Chinese and Malay architecture grafted onto the traditional houses built by Broome's pearling masters.*

Below: *The Geikie Gorge National Park in the Kimberley region contains limestone walls that are a gallery of marine fossils from the time when this area was a seabed.*

Above: *Since they appeared on Australian television in the 1980s, the sandstone domes of the Bungle Bungle Range in Purnululu National Park have become as famous as their cousins, Uluru and Katatjuta.*

Overleaf: *Lake Argyle is surrounded by the hills of the Carr–Boyd Range near Kununurra in the state's north-west. The lake, created by damming the Ord River, is the reservoir for the giant Ord River irrigation scheme.*

SOUTH AUSTRALIA

Adelaide, the capital of South Australia, is a city of style and character brimming with history. Ringed by parklands and well-furnished with gardens, fountains, squares and broad avenues, Adelaide also knows how to have a good time. The vineyards that surround it produce some of Australia's finest wines and the outdoor cafes along Rundle Street bring a continental flavour to the heart of the city. Adelaide also prides itself on its cultural attainments and the Adelaide Festival brings international artists of drama, music, dance and literature to town for a glittering celebration of contemporary arts and culture.

South Australia is rich in attractions as diverse as the spicy taste of a Clare Valley shiraz, the thunder of a whale heaving itself from the Great Southern Ocean and the tortured, primeval splendour of the Flinders Ranges. Inland is Lake Eyre, a great salt lake that rarely fills with water – the last time was in 1989, only the third time in recorded history.

Above: *The stately Adelaide Casino is housed in the building that served for many years as the city's central railway station.*

Left: *The Glenelg Tram runs along Adelaide's last surviving tramline; it provides a link between the city and the beachside suburb.*

Opposite: *Rocks form an arch at Bales Bay to frame the south coast cliffs of Kangaroo Island, Australia's third largest island.*

Left: *The beachside at Glenelg is particularly favoured by Adelaide residents.*

Right: *The Bicentennial Conservatory houses tropical plants from around the world and strikes a bold pose in Adelaide's magnificent Botanic Gardens.*

Left: *Australian sea lions frequent the beach at Kangaroo Island's Seal Bay, an area almost totally unaffected by humans.*

Opposite: *Vineyards and date palms at Seppeltsfield are among the most spectacular and best tended in the Barossa Valley. The area was founded by immigrants fleeing religious persecution in Silesia.*

Below: *Chateau Yaldara in the Barossa stands testament to the proud traditions of hard work and solid architecture bequeathed by the original German settlers.*

Above: *The Remarkable Rocks lie scattered like giant bones on Kirkpatrick Point in the Flinders Chase National Park at the western edge of Kangaroo Island.*

Below: *Cape de Couedic lighthouse at the south-western extremity of Kangaroo Island assists boats navigating these difficult waters.*

Coober Pedy

Left: *These opals belong to the collection in the Opal Cave at Coober Pedy, where miners still guard their leases jealously and trespassers can be fined.*

Right: *The Opal Cave not only provides a social history of the area, but also gives an in-depth look at the mining and engineering feats that have created Coober Pedy.*

Below and bottom: *Coober Pedy's Aboriginal meaning is 'white fella's hole', a direct reference to the houses, motels, churches and shops built underground to escape the summer heat. These dwellings offer an insight into the remarkable characters who call them 'home'.*

VICTORIA

The capital of Victoria and Australia's second largest metropolis, Melbourne is a serene, gracious city of dazzling parks, cool-climate gardens, tree-lined boulevards, cafes, bookshops and trams – a city that inspires comparisons with Europe more than any other Australian state capital. Both Melbourne and Victoria prospered mightily from the gold rush of the mid-1800s, as the flamboyant Victorian architecture testifies. Victoria's capital is also known in horse-racing circles around the world as the home of the Melbourne Cup – an event for which the entire nation pauses.

Victoria is the smallest mainland state but includes a wealth of natural and man-made wonders, including the Great Ocean Road, the most spectacular coastal drive in the country; glorious goldmining towns with a history written in sweat and toil; cool-climate vineyards; fishing villages that began life as whaling towns; and the majestic high country, an inspiration for writers and painters and anyone who enjoys a walk in the clouds.

Above: Tour boats await customers on the Yarra River, while just a few kilometres upstream the river flows through the green glories of Studley Park.

Below: Melbourne trams are solid, dependable and eminently practical; they have also become part of the very essence of the city.

Above: Flinders Street Station, built when Melbourne was at the peak of its prosperity, shows the fine traditions of Victorian style.

Left: A sculpted figure gazes to the heavens, perhaps in awe of the handsome Southgate complex, the newest and most glamorous addition to the city's architecture.

Opposite: Melbourne's skyline from the south bank of the Yarra displays the elegance of this gracious yet modern city.

Above: *Built in 1869, the Royal Arcade evokes the time when Melbourne was flush with money from the goldfields of Victoria. The figures flanking the clock are Gog and Magog, favourite bogey-men from every Melbourne childhood.*

Opposite: *An aerial view of Melbourne shows the latticework tower of the Performing Arts Centre, the Southgate complex on the left bank of the river, the railway lines radiating from Flinders Street Station, and the business district of the city.*

Above: *The British Raj-style Exhibition Buildings, at the heart of Carlton Gardens north-east of Melbourne, were constructed for the International Exhibition of 1880.*

Below left: *Captain Cook's Cottage was transported stone by stone from Yorkshire and rebuilt in Melbourne's Fitzroy Gardens.*

Below: *Cafes spill across the pavement in Lygon Street, a favourite Melbourne haunt brimming with Mediterranean eateries.*

Above and below: *Fairy penguins emerge from their shelter and prepare to march to the sea across the beach at Phillip Island, where crowds await the parade. The penguins, which have become one of the most frequented tourist attractions in the state, spend the entire day at sea, returning to their burrows in the evening.*

Right: *The Puffing Billy is a perennial crowd-pleaser as it makes its stately progress through the magnificent forests of the Dandenong Ranges, east of Melbourne. The train steams along a 13km-long narrow-gauge line from Belgrave to Emerald Lake; once a year runners on foot challenge the Billy in the Great Train Race.*

Right: *The Grampians National Park in central Victoria is known for its breathtaking scenery. An out-crop near Reid Lookout provides a perfect vantage point.*

Above: *Autumn casts a warm glow across the ranges at Halls Gap in the Grampians. These richly forested sandstone ranges are a natural wonderland for bushwalkers, climbers and wildlife watchers.*

Below: *Shopfronts at Ballarat's Sovereign Hill create an authentic rendition of life, work and play on the Victorian gold diggings in the 1850s. This area is where most of Australia's gold was found.*

Above: *Beautiful, colourful begonias are cultivated in a glasshouse at Ballarat; the annual Begonia Festival is one of the highlights of this handsome Victorian city, once a goldmining centre.*

Opposite: *The limestone sentinels of the Twelve Apostles guard the southern Victorian coastline. The Great Ocean Road, which borders this coastline, is the most spectacular coastal drive in the country.*

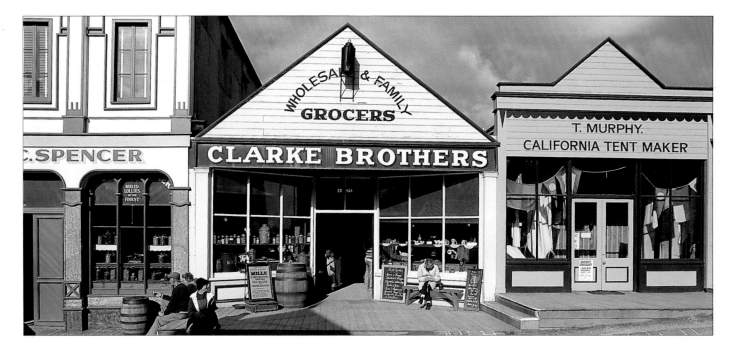

Far left: *The Foot of the Horn at Mount Buffalo National Park, where granite bluffs tower 1000m above the Ovens Valley of north-eastern Victoria, is open to snow skiers during winter, and in spring, becomes a wonderland for hikers when wildflowers carpet the ranges.*

Left: *A wedge-tailed eagle, Australia's largest bird of prey with a wingspan of about 2.5m, soars above the ranges of northern Victoria.*

Above: *Ninety Mile Beach stretches along Victoria's south-eastern coast, a summer paradise for boating and fishing enthusiasts. Behind the beach lie the Gippsland Lakes.*

Right: *Fishing boats moor at Lakes Entrance, where the vast complex of the Gippsland Lakes, the country's largest network of inland waterways, spills into the sea.*

Opposite: *Sunset brings a reflective mood to Lakes Entrance, home to a large shipping fleet. Lakes Entrance also boasts a shell museum, an antique car museum and an Aboriginal art museum. The Buchan Caves are located nearby.*

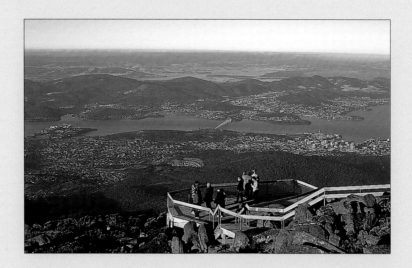

TASMANIA

Tasmania's European history began early in the 19th century when several penal colonies were established to house Sydney's worst offenders. Today, the island's convict-built churches and bridges are among its most treasured sites. Nestled on a magnificent harbour at the foot of Mount Wellington is Hobart, the capital and the second oldest city in the country. It has a colourful history and a modern outlook, with Georgian buildings and historic suburbs happily residing next to new complexes like the foreshore's Wrest Point Hotel–Casino.

To mainland Australians, Tasmania belongs to another time – a slower, friendlier past when drivers waved at one another and nobody locked their front door. While Tasmania is often depicted by scenes of willow-lined streams and velvet-green pastures evoking the English countryside, the island is also spectacularly rugged. So dense and forbidding are its forests that parts of the south-west have never been explored.

Above: Hobart, set on the estuary of the Derwent River, can be seen in its full glory from the heights of Mount Wellington.

Right: Salamanca Markets is the place to shop for arts and crafts, and to hear the local street musicians.

Left: Cascade Brewery is the oldest in Australia and still produces a highly regarded ale.

Right: Constitution Dock comes alive every year when the fliers of the Sydney to Hobart Ocean Yacht Race near the finishing line.

Opposite: Cradle Mountain–Lake St Clair National Park, with its open moors, mountains and the picturesque Lake Lilla, is a wilderness paradise.

Above: *The thickset, forest-dwelling wombat uses its powerful front claws to dig deep burrows, making it extremely unpopular with farmers and horseriders.*

Opposite: *The Gordon River snakes through the forests of the Franklin–Gordon Wild Rivers National Park on the island's west coast.*

Above: *The wilderness tracks between Mole Creek and Cradle Mountain show why some of the dense forests in the south-west have never been explored on foot.*

Below: *Sorell is one of the oldest towns in the state and its Barracks, built in 1823, show the solid, unadorned style that typified the early architecture of Tasmania. Sorell was an important wheat-growing region for the early colony, and a 3300m-long causeway was built across the Pitt Water in 1872.*

Below: *This convict-built church is located at Port Arthur, about 100km from Hobart. Port Arthur was founded as a penal colony for the very worst convict offenders and witnessed terrifying brutality.*

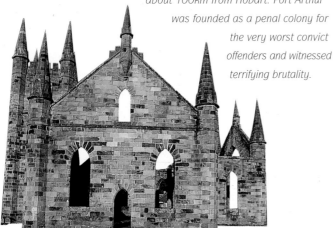

Freycinet National Park is a wild, wind-swept peninsula on Tasmania's east coast.

First published in 1997 by
New Holland Publishers (Australia) Pty Ltd
Sydney • London • Cape Town

14 Aquatic Drive
Frenchs Forest NSW 2086
Australia

24 Nutford Place
London W1H 6DQ
United Kingdom

80 McKenzie Street
Cape Town 8001
South Africa

Copyright © 1997 New Holland Publishers (Australia) Pty Ltd
Copyright © 1997 in text: Michael Gebicki
Copyright © 1997 in maps: New Holland Publishers (Australia) Pty Ltd
Copyright © 1997 in photographs: photographers and/or their
agents as listed below.

Reprinted 1998

ISBN 1 86436 222 7

Writer: Michael Gebicki
Commissioning editors: Averill Chase, Sally Bird
Concept designer: Alix Gracie
Cover designer: Lyndall Hamilton
Senior designer: Peter Bosman
Editors: Joanne Holliman, Anouska Good
Typesetter: Gerda Pretorius
DTP cartographer: John Loubser
Picture Research: Vicki Hastrich

Reproduction by cmyk prepress
Printed and bound in Singapore by Tien Wah Press (Pte) Ltd

Photographic Acknowledgements

Copyright © in photographs: **NHIL** (Shaen Adey) with the exception of the following:
Kevin Deacon/Ocean Earth Images: p43; **M. Gebicki**: pp2 (top), 42 (right centre); **NHIL** (Denise Greig): p6 (bottom left); **NHIL**: front cover (background & etch), pp8 (top), 13 (top), 44 (top), 71, 74 (top left & centre); **NHIL** (Anthony Johnson): front cover (top left), pp1, 6 (etch & left centre), 10 (etch), 11 (etch & bottom right), 14 (etch & bottom right), 17 (top), 21, 28, 30 (etch & left centre), 31, 32, 33 (top & etch), 38 (top), 39, 40–41, 42 (top & bottom left), 44 (bottom), 46, 47 (left centre & bottom right), 50–51, 50 (centre), 51 (bottom left, centre & bottom right), 52 (centre), 60 (left centre & bottom, & etch), 66, 67 (top, left, right & etch), 68, 69 (top left & right, bottom left & right), 77 (etch), 79, back cover (etch); **NHIL** (Nick Rains): pp10 (bottom left), 12 (top), 22, 23 (bottom centre & right); **Dave Watts**: pp6 (top right & bottom right), 48 (etch), 70 (top), 74 (etch), 78 (top right).